Baby Animals

SCHOLASTIC INC.
New York Toronto London
Auckland Sydney Mexico City
New Delhi Hong Kong

In the snow

Arctic fox

My *furry* paws and **thick** coat mean I can walk in the snow to find food.

Crunch crunch!

Snow monkey

I live in very cold temperatures, so I like to swim in hot springs when I get the chance.

Splish splash!

Penguin

I stay **Cozy** underneath my mom and dad and wait for them to bring me food.

SnUggle!

Snow leopard

I have lots of fluffy fur and a *long* tail that I use to keep my face warm when I'm asleep. zzz

PuuUrrrrrr!

Polar bear

My paws are large so I can walk on snow and thin ice without falling through — they also help me swim.

Grrrrrr!

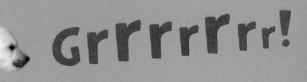

Arctic wolf

When I grow up, my fur will be pure white so that I'm harder to spot in the snow.

HOOOWWWW!!!

Seal

At first I drink milk from my mom, but soon I'll start eating tasty fish.

Yum yum!

ISBN 978-0-545-39343-0

12 11 10 9 8 7 6 5 4 3 2   11 12 13 14 15 16/0

Printed in the U.S.A.   40

First Scholastic printing, September 2011

Photo Credits
Every care has been taken to trace copyright holders.

Cover, 1: Photolibrary/Wayne Lynch; 2 Alamy/Picture Contact;
3 Alamy/Richard Codington; 4 Alamy/Natural Visions; 5 Alamy/Danita Delimont;
6 Photolibrary; 7 Photolibrary/Thorsten Milse; 8 Corbis/Klaus-Dietmar Gabbert;
9 Photolibrary/Philip Tull; 10 Alamy/Juniors Bildarchiv; 11 Alamy/Alaska Stock;
12 FLPA/Jim Brandenburg/Minden; 13 NaturePL/Jeff Turner;
14 Photolibrary/Wayne Lynch; 15 Photolibrary/Wayne Lynch